Shelly Bean the Sports Queen

Plays Basketball

By Shelly Boyum-Breen

Illustrated by Marieka Heinlen

DeDicaTioN: This book belongs to all young sports fans that love to play, work hard, try new things, and dream big. When I was six, I dreamed of playing in the NBA, NHL, NFL and MLB. I worked hard to make my dreams come true, and I made many friends and memories along the way. While I did not end up playing professional sports, I did do a lot of other cool things with my life—like write these books for kids! I am active every day and eager to share my passion for playing sports with others. My hope is that Shelly Bean inspires YOU to play.

AcKnowLeDgEmEnTs: A special thank-you to my youth coaches, parents, brothers, spouse, children, nephews and nieces and many friends who have supported me as I've grown as an athlete and as the creator of Shelly Bean the Sports Queen. Finally, an enormous "thank you" to the "backers" and Team Bean who worked creatively as a unit to help bring Shelly Bean to life.

PUBLISHED BY:
Level Field Press, LLC
2960 Everest Lane
Plymouth, MN 55447
shellybeanthesportsqueen.com

Illustrated By: Marieka Meinlen
Design & Print Production:
Blue Tricycle, Inc.

Boyum-Breen, Shelly.
   Shelly Bean the Sports Queen plays basketball / by Shelly Boyum-Breen ; illustrated by Marieka Heinlen.
    pages cm
   SUMMARY: Shelly Bean the Sports Queen learns about friendship and team spirit while playing basketball.
   Audience: Grade 2.
   ISBN 978-1-4951-1492-2

   1. Basketball for girls--Juvenile fiction. 2. Team sports--Juvenile fiction. [1. Basketball for girls--Fiction. 2. Sports for girls--Fiction. 3. Team sports --Fiction. 4. Friendship--Fiction.]   I. Heinlen, Marieka, illustrator. II. Title.

PZ7.B6972Shpb 2014   [E]
                QBI14-600109

Team Shelly Bean

Shelly Bean loves to try new sports and she wants you to try new sports too! Let's see what she learns to play today. Then follow the tips at the end of the book and start playing with her!

Spike
co-mascot

Buster
co-mascot

Shelly Bean
the Sports Queen

Ben
bigger brother

Maya
best buddy

Matt
big brother

One sunny day, Shelly Bean was playing in the backyard with her dog Spike when she heard the sound of a basketball bouncing nearby. Boing! Boing! It sure sounded fun.

She ran out to the curb and saw her friends Maya and Mason playing basketball. Shelly ran over to join them and Spike couldn't wait to see his friend Buster!

The basketball left Mason's hand and went **Swoosh!** through the net.

Shelly Bean tried to copy Mason, but it wasn't even close. Then Maya tried, and her shot went over the basket.

Shelly Bean watched and listened closely to Mason as he gave some good advice.

Pretend your arm is a goose's neck and your hand is its head, like this. Then, let the ball roll off your fingertips.

I think I get it.

Shelly did just as Mason said, and this time the ball tapped the backboard and dropped through the hoop!

A few neighborhood kids and Shelly's brothers even stopped to see what was going on. Shelly Bean really felt great.

"WhooOOOO-Hooo!",
yelled Maya and Mason.

"I know what would be fun", said Mason. "Let's play DUNK!"
Shelly Bean couldn't wait to learn a new game, but Maya
wasn't so sure.

Mason explained the rules of DUNK.

Rules of DUNK

1. Take a shot and if you make it, then other players have to make it from the same spot.

2. If they miss, they get letter D for DUNK.

3. If they make it, they get to pick the next spot.

4. The first one to spell DUNK is out of the game.

5. The last one in the game wins!

After taking several turns,
Mason had D,
Shelly Bean had a D-U,
and Maya had a D-U-N.

One more miss and Maya
was out of the game.

Maya was frustrated, but Shelly refused to
let her best friend give up.

"It just takes practice. Remember how hard it
was for me to learn how to skate last winter?
I fell down tons of times!"

Maya gave it another try. This time she got really close, but the ball rolled around the rim of the hoop and fell off the side.

"Try shooting with just one hand, Maya. It's easier to get a good arch in your throw."

Only Shelly Bean and Mason were left in the game. Shelly made a great shot but Mason missed. "Uh oh!" said Mason. "I spelled DUNK so you win Shelly Bean!"

Maya was ready to be done.

"Maybe I'll have a better game tomorrow," sighed Maya, throwing the ball over her shoulder.

Swish! Sloop! Maya made a basket without looking!

They all laughed. "Learning a new sport together is super fun," thought Shelly.

Shelly realized she could practice shooting baskets anywhere, even the laundry room. Tissues in the trash! Towel in the hamper!

Uh-OH! Shelly Bean's towel landed on her dad's head instead.

After bath time, Shelly looked up at the posters in her room and thought maybe one day there will be a poster of her playing basketball up there.

Shelly Bean made a new basketball charm and carefully placed it on her crown of sports.

I am Shelly Bean the Sports Queen!

Shelly Bean placed the crown on her head, stood tall in front of her mirror and thought, "I wonder what awesome sport I'll learn next?"

Tips for Learning to Play Basketball

These tips are written for a right-handed shooter. Left-handed shooters should simply use the opposite hand or foot stated below.

1. Stand about 5 feet in front of the basketball hoop with your feet shoulder width apart and knees slightly bent for balance. Bend your upper body slightly at the hips.

2. Hold the ball in your "shooting hand" with the ball resting on the tips of your fingers. The palm of your hand should point to the sky. Your pointer finger should be pointing backwards at your right eye.

3. Your right elbow should be away from your body and over your right foot.

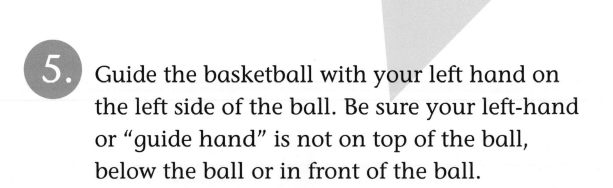

4. Hold the basketball about chin height.

5. Guide the basketball with your left hand on the left side of the ball. Be sure your left-hand or "guide hand" is not on top of the ball, below the ball or in front of the ball.

6. Using your legs for power, push the basketball up towards the sky and towards the basket. Your right elbow should finish by your right ear.

7. "Snap" your right wrist down to the ground as the ball rolls off your fingertips.

8. You should finish your "follow-through" with your shooting arm fully extended high in the air, your elbow by your ear and your wrist snapped down. Imagine your arm is the neck of a goose, your hand is the head and your fingers are the beak.

9. Keep repeating this motion starting back at step 1 until you are able to make 10 baskets. When you are able to make 10, move back another five feet from the basket and repeat the steps again.

How many baskets can you make in a row?

Glossary

Basket: A metal hoop with a net attached. Players try to throw the basketball through the net to score points.

Offense: The team with control of the ball. They are trying to shoot the ball into the basket.

Defense: The team without control of the ball. They are trying to prevent the other team from making baskets.

Field Goal: Scored when a player shoots the ball through the basket. It is usually worth 2 points. But it's worth 3 points if the shooter is standing behind the 3-point line.

Dunk: When a player jumps up close to the basket and throws the ball hard through it.

Dribble: When a player bounces the ball on the floor with one hand as she moves down the basketball court.

Pass: When a player throws the ball to a teammate.

About the Author

Shelly Boyum-Breen grew up playing sports in her neighborhood with friends, her brothers and on her school teams. She found that the life-long benefits of sports for girls were so important that she needed to write this series and inspire girls across the world to play. Shelly resides in Minnesota with her spouse, has two adult daughters and continues to play sports and be active.

About the Illustrator

After designing books and working as a creative director in publishing, Marieka made the leap to become a children's book illustrator. Now with over 30 picture books in print, she loves creating artwork that engages and educates young readers. Marieka always aims to draw an environment where all children can see themselves, as well as the big wonderful world around them.

More action packed books in this Series:

- **Shelly Bean the Sports Queen Skates at the Hockey Rink**

- **Shelly Bean the Sports Queen Plays a Game of Catch**

- **Shelly Bean the Sports Queen Plays Basketball**

   And many more…